GW00418984

ON YOUR

WEDDING

ON YOUR WEDDING

Summersdale Publishers Ltd
46 West Street
Chichester
West Sussex
PO19 1RP
UK

www.summersdale.com

Printed and bound in China

ISBN: 978-1-84953-423-9

Substantial discounts on bulk quantities of Summersdale books are available to corporations, professional associations and other organisations. For details contact Nicky Douglas by telephone: +44 (0) 1243 756902, fax: +44 (0) 1243 786300 or email: nicky@summersdale.com.

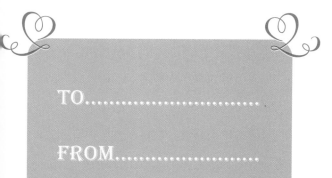

TO............................

FROM.........................

Weddings to me
are wondrous
because they are
so filled with
tomorrows.

MARY FORSELL

The highest
happiness on
earth is
marriage.

WILLIAM LYON PHELPS

The real act of
marriage takes
place in the heart,
not in the ballroom
or church or
synagogue.

BARBARA DE ANGELIS

Having a place to go – is a home. Having someone to love – is a family. Having both – is a blessing.

DONNA HEDGES

Whatever our

SOULS

are made of,

HIS and MINE are the SAME.

EMILY BRONTË

Are we not like two
volumes of one book?

MARCELINE DESBORDES-VALMORE

Love does not consist of gazing at each other, but in looking together in the same direction.

ANTOINE DE SAINT-EXUPÉRY

LOVE IS COMPOSED
OF A SINGLE SOUL
INHABITING TWO
BODIES.

ARISTOTLE

There is no
such cosy
combination as
man and wife.

MENANDER

Marriage is the perfection of what love is aimed at.

RALPH WALDO EMERSON

Have a heart that
never hardens, a
temper that never
tires, a touch that
never hurts.

CHARLES DICKENS

No jealousy their dawn of love overcast, nor blasted were their wedded days with strife; each season looked delightful as it past, to the fond husband and the faithful wife.

JAMES BEATTIE

Desire looks clear
from the eyes of a
lovely bride: power
as strong as the
founded world.

SOPHOCLES

After all there is
something about
a wedding-gown
prettier than in
any other gown in
the world.

DOUGLAS WILLIAM JERROLD

A WOMAN SELDOM ASKS ADVICE BEFORE SHE HAS BOUGHT HER WEDDING CLOTHES.

JOSEPH ADDISON

I think men who have
a pierced ear are
better prepared for
marriage. They've
experienced pain and
bought jewellery.

RITA RUDNER

True love stories
never have
endings.

RICHARD BACH

I LOVE THEE to the depth and breadth and height

MY SOUL

can reach.

ELIZABETH BARRETT BROWNING

The first thing I did when I sold my book was to buy a new wedding ring for my wife and asked her to marry me all over again.

NICHOLAS SPARKS

Love recognises no barriers. It jumps hurdles, leaps fences, penetrates walls to arrive at its destination full of hope.

MAYA ANGELOU

You come to love not
by finding the perfect
person, but by seeing
an imperfect person
perfectly.

SAM KEEN

You have my
whole heart for my
whole life.

FRENCH PROVERB

WE LOVE BECAUSE
IT'S THE ONLY TRUE
ADVENTURE.

NIKKI GIOVANNI

The world is too dangerous for anything but truth and too small for anything but love.

WILLIAM SLOANE COFFIN

Marriages
are made in
heaven.

ENGLISH PROVERB

A person's character is but half formed till after wedlock.

CHARLES SIMMONS

Getting married,
for me, was the
best thing I
ever did.

NICK CAVE

Marriage: that I call
the will of two to
create the one who is
more than those who
created it.

FRIEDRICH NIETZSCHE

Marriage is not just spiritual communion, it is also remembering to take out the trash.

JOYCE BROTHERS

IF I GET MARRIED,
I WANT TO BE
VERY MARRIED.

AUDREY HEPBURN

O MONTH

when they

WHO LOVE

must

LOVE and WED.

HELEN HUNT JACKSON

By all means marry;
if you get a good wife,
you'll become happy;
if you get a bad one,
you'll become a
philosopher.

SOCRATES

Love is smiling on the inside and out.

JENNIFER WILLIAMS

Marriage is an
alliance entered
into by a man who
can't sleep with
the window shut,
and a woman who
can't sleep with
the window open.

GEORGE BERNARD SHAW

I sing of
maypoles, hockcarts,
wassails, wakes,
Of bridegrooms,
brides, and of their
bridal cakes.

ROBERT HERRICK

This ring the
Bride-groom did for
none provide
But for his bride.

HENRY VAUGHAN

Weddings are not over until they are sealed with a kiss.

SUSAN MARG

IN ALL OF THE WEDDING
CAKE, HOPE IS THE
SWEETEST OF PLUMS.

DOUGLAS JERROLD

If you can survive
the wedding, they
say, the rest is a
piece of cake.

NOAH HAWLEY

Now join your hands, and with your hands your hearts.

WILLIAM SHAKESPEARE

Love is a symbol of
eternity. It wipes
out all sense of
time, destroying
all memory of a
beginning and all
fear of an end.

MADAME DE STAËL

There is only one
happiness in life —
to love and be loved.

GEORGE SAND

Two souls with but a
single thought,
Two hearts that beat
as one!

FRIEDRICH HALM

EVERYTHING
is clearer

when you're
IN LOVE.

JOHN LENNON

What we find
in a soulmate is
not something
wild to tame but
something wild to
run with.

ROBERT BRAULT

WE CAN ONLY
LEARN TO LOVE
BY LOVING.

IRIS MURDOCH

We have the greatest
prenuptial agreement
in the world.
It's called love.

GENE PERRET

Paradise is
always where
love dwells.

JEAN PAUL

To be fully seen
by somebody,
then, and be loved
anyhow – this is
a human offering
that can border on
miraculous.

ELIZABETH GILBERT

If two stand
shoulder to shoulder
against the gods,
Happy together, the
gods themselves
are helpless...

MAXWELL ANDERSON

There's a higher
form of happiness in
commitment.

CLAIRE FORLANI

For two people
in a marriage
to live together
day after day is
unquestionably
the one miracle
the Vatican has
overlooked.

BILL COSBY

THE BEST THING TO
HOLD ONTO IN LIFE
IS EACH OTHER.

AUDREY HEPBURN

Weddings remind us
that our lives have
meaning and that love
is the strongest bond...

DAPHNE ROSE KINGMA

... love heals everything, and love is all there is.

GARY ZUKAV

I have always considered marriage as the most interesting event of one's life, the foundation of happiness.

GEORGE WASHINGTON

One of the secrets
of life is that all
that is really
worth the doing
is what we
do for others.

LEWIS CARROLL

Our eyes first give
birth to love, and
our hearts give it
sustenance.

GIACOMO DA LENTINI

What does love feel like?

INCREDIBLE.

REBECCA ADLINGTON

If you press me to say why I loved him, I can say no more than because he was he, and I was I.

MICHEL DE MONTAIGNE

LOVE IS LIKE DEW
THAT FALLS ON BOTH
NETTLES AND LILIES.

SWEDISH PROVERB

Love endures only
when the lovers love
many things together
and not merely
each other.

WALTER LIPPMANN

Love is a
friendship set
to music.

ELI JOSEPH COSSMAN

Love must be as
much a light as it
is a flame.

HENRY DAVID THOREAU

Grow old along
with me!
The best is
yet to be...

ROBERT BROWNING

Sometimes the heart
sees what is invisible
to the eye.

H. JACKSON BROWN JR

[He is] quite simply my strength and stay.

THE QUEEN, ON PRINCE PHILIP

A HEART THAT
LOVES IS
ALWAYS YOUNG.

GREEK PROVERB

Come, let's be a
comfortable couple
and take care of
each other!

CHARLES DICKENS

There is no instinct like that of the heart.

LORD BYRON

Where love is
concerned, too
much is not
even enough.

PIERRE BEAUMARCHAIS

Lust is easy. Love is
hard. Like is most
important.

CARL REINER

Let all thy joys be as
the month of May,
And all thy days be as
a marriage day.

FRANCIS QUARLES

Here's to the
HAPPY
MAN:

All the
world loves
A LOVER.

RALPH WALDO EMERSON

A wedding anniversary is the celebration of love, trust, partnership, tolerance and tenacity. The order varies for any given year.

PAUL SWEENEY

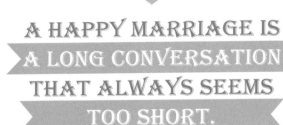

A HAPPY MARRIAGE IS
A LONG CONVERSATION
THAT ALWAYS SEEMS
TOO SHORT.

ANDRÉ MAUROIS

When we are in love
we seem to ourselves
quite different from
what we were before.

BLAISE PASCAL

Never go to bed mad. Stay up and fight.

PHYLLIS DILLER

But to see her was to love her, love but her, and love forever.

ROBERT BURNS

A good husband
makes a good wife.

JOHN FLORIO

A good marriage is
at least 80 per cent
good luck in finding
the right person at the
right time. The rest
is trust.

NANETTE NEWMAN

Love is everything
it's cracked up
to be... worth
fighting for, being
brave for, risking
everything for.

ERICA JONG

IF I KNOW WHAT
LOVE IS, IT IS
BECAUSE OF YOU.

HERMANN HESSE

I am in love – and, my God, it's the greatest thing that can happen to a man.

D. H. LAWRENCE

Where there is love there is no question.

ALBERT EINSTEIN

A successful
marriage requires
falling in love
many times,
always with the
same person.

MIGNON MCLAUGHLIN

If you're interested in finding
out more about our books,
find us on Facebook at
Summersdale Publishers
and follow us on Twitter at
@Summersdale

WWW.SUMMERSDALE.COM